honey
and
vinegar

and a little something in between

honey and vinegar
and a little something in between

poetry by
janis nicole townsend

§

Copyright © 2008 by Janis Nicole Townsend

All rights reserved.

This book is a work of fiction. Names, characters, places and incidents are products of the author's imagination or are used fictitiously. Any resemblance to actual events or locales or persons, living or dead, is entirely coincidental.

Printed in the United States of America.

First Edition

ISBN: 978-0-615-26115-7

No part of this book may be reproduced or transmitted in any form or by any means, electronic or mechanical, including photocopying, recording, or by any information storage and retrieval system, without expressed permission of the author/publisher.

Artwork:

Front cover painting "One Love" by Janis Nicole Townsend

Jacket design D. Badger www.bookwormdesigns.com

Photograph on back cover by Mr. 100

thank you.

this book is dedicated to the people that i have loved the most along the way, and had to lose to become the me that i am today…

love yourself and teach others to love themselves
and we all learn how to truly love each other

and to the very few who overstand:
no space or time
we exist beyond words

Acknowledgments

Acknowledgments aren't easy... Not because I wouldn't know who to acknowledge or what to say but because there have been so many influential people in my life—who do I leave out?

In an effort to make the book about the poetry, I want to acknowledge some people who have been pivotal in my life as it pertains to my work. These people have in some way; shape or form liberated me, through inspiration via their art form, their lifestyle, or our direct interactions. Many people fall into that category but some of the more famous names are Jay-Z, Sonia Sanchez, Nikki Giovanni, Nina Simone, Billie Holiday, Bob Marley, Jewel, Alicia Keys, Paulo Coelho, Kahlil Gibran, Kevin Liles, Don Miguel Ruiz, Ne-Yo, Steve Stoute, Iyanla Vanzant, Tupac, Saul Williams, Lisa Price, Lenny Kravitz, Jada Pinkett-Smith, Mary J. Blige, Maj Toure and so many others. Their words, their careers, their stories, have enriched my journey in ways I could never truly explain so I will only say—thank you for sharing your life with me through your hard work, I am sure you all have saved my life many times over.

To my friends and family—there are so many of you! Where would I begin? The Townsend and Gresham families as a whole... You all make life worth living! Thank you to Hanna Kim, and Denine Labat for proof reading and providing early feedback on the manuscript for me. Thanks to David for taking all my bitching when it came to the jacket design.

Many years ago, I met a woman named Madeline Nelson and my whole life changed. Somehow, I began to have direction in my life and hope for my future. My dreams used to be too big for my mind to wrap around and believe in and I was afraid to go after them. Maddi, through example, opened the window to the possibility that there was more to life than that limited way of thinking and made me believe that I could actually obtain my goals through planning, hard work and prayer. Truly, without her—this book would still be in a journal, as would the rest of my hopes.

Many thanks to my parents: Lisa Townsend and Bill Townsend, for obvious reasons! (Smile.)

And, thank you, to the woman who created the frame and foundation of my life, my grandmother, Ida W. Townsend.

I love you Grandmom.

Her response from heaven:
"Nicole, baby, you know I love you too… but you know I love all my kids and my grandkids…"

We miss you.

book opener...

I want to fill the pages of my book
Leave no page untouched
For loneliness weighs heavy on my heart
And seeing a blank page is just too much
My heart can't take it as I look
So, my hand begins to write
No more lonely pages or sad faces
My pen came prepared to fight
Fight for the right to write without reason
The right to write for no cause
The right to write wrongs and rights for
Simply no reason @ all
Except for maybe the simple fact
My heart doesn't want to have an attack
And can't stand to see bare naked pages
Just because a couple of words they lack
So, I will write to save myself
And to save my lovely book too
From a death sentence of a lonely life
Because, you know, it's just us two.

nicole.

Table of Contents

1. Acknowledgments: vii
2. book opener: ix

chapter one: never give up on love...

1. i was in love: 3
2. waiting: 4
3. love poem 1: 5
4. love poem 2: 6
5. emotional conquest: 7
6. is it a sin? : 8
7. i'm special: 9
8. reminders: 10
9. love poem 3: 11
10. plea of insanity: 12
11. love poem 4: 13
12. blue moon: 14
13. yet again: 15
14. not his type: 16
15. letter to my last love: 17
16. not a dream: 18
17. i hate you: 19
18. love poem 5: 20
19. pain: 21
20. the end: 22
21. cliffhanger: 23
22. keyboard: 24

chapter two: when did you see the butterflies again...

1. a woman's mind (behind the mystery): 27
2. fool: 28
3. past: 29
4. maybe: 30
5. borrowed love: 31
6. i need you: 32
7. oprah episode: 33

8. mr. right: 34
9. crush: 35
10. innocence: 36
11. patience: 37
12. i want you: 38
13. sleep: 39
14. butterflies and caterpillars: 40
15. i am in love: 41
16. if: 43
17. your love: 44
18. happy birthday: 45
19. bliss: 46
20. simple: 47
21. dreaming: 48

chapter 3: a gallon of rocky road...

1. raped: 51
2. 30 minutes, press start: 52
3. insane: 53
4. suicide gone wrong: 54
5. where am i?: 56
6. suicidal tendencies: 57
7. a gallon of rocky road...: 58
8. trials of love: 59
9. changing the pillowcase...: 60
10. remembering love: 61
11. not so many words: 62
12. release (multiple times): 63
13. truthfully: 64
14. same difference: 65
15. thoughts on focus: 66
16. not naïve: 67
17. thoughts on relations: 68
18. thoughts on money and people: 69
19. i don't know how to write a poem anymore: 70

chapter 4: singing in the shower

    1. singing in the shower: 73
    2. time: 74
    3. optimism: 75
    4. live: 76
    5. breath control: 77
    6. happiness: 78
    7. passionate: 79
    8. sunny days: 80
    9. zonin': 81
    10. deception: 82
    11. tanka (ten percent): 83
    12. tanka (sour grapes): 84
    13. tanka (naïve): 85
    14. tanka (mr. belvedere): 86
    15. tanka (we have dreams): 87
    16. tanka (hurricane season): 88
    17. (1): 89
    18. haiku (hate): 90

chapter 5: if the walls could talk…

    1. mental stimulation: 93
    2. golden sandalwood: 95
    3. love @ 1st sight: 97
    4. warning label: 99
    5. déjà vu: 101
    6. translucent: 103
    7. is she gone foreva?: 104
    8. soul mate: 106
    9. our story: 107
    10. a poem for you, brooklyn: 109
    11. fuck you: 110
    12. i just need you: 112
    13. he called: 114
    14. ricky: 117
    15. lovers: 119
    16. i wanna be a poet: 120

thank you: 123

chapter 1

never give up on love…

I Was In Love

Some time ago,
I was in love.

Though still a child,
I knew I was in love.

One night he called me late,
To myself I thought, "I am in love!"

He told me he liked my friend more than me,
I knew I *was* in love.

Waiting…

I hate the feeling of waiting
for someone to call.
They never do.
So, I say, "If anyone calls
I don't want to speak to them…
No one!"

No one calls.

So, I want to call and say,
"Don't call me ever again!"

So, I won't be waiting.
So, I can sleep.
So, I can say,
"….so, I told him not to call
me anymore—because I was sick of it!"

But, still no calls,
and I'm still waiting…

Love Poem 1

The story of my life…
cry, cry, cry
Why?
One minute I think I'm
in love
The next minute I know
I am
because he's not here
and I'm missing everything,
and the worst thing of all
is to actually realize
I'm feeling this all
by myself

One sided love.

Love Poem 2

The light of my love
for you
Shines so bright
that it blinds me
So much that I don't
see your light go out
I can't stand this light
it hurts my eyes

but

I'm afraid of the dark.

Emotional Conquest

Why do you play with my mind?
Is it on purpose?
Do you set out to run through my emotions
like a roller coaster?
Do you even know what you do to me?
Do you envision me sitting here
writing blurriness with teary eyes
knowing that tomorrow I'll smile
and never tell…
I'll just sit, listen to excuses,
say I understand.
Be your ultimate superwoman,
tell you it's alright that you
were too busy to call,
I mean, after all—
you have priorities right?

Is it a Sin?

It's so nice to feel wanted
To feel *special* even
"Call me in the morning
When you wake up"
Almost touched heaven
Until I realized—it wasn't you
But even you can't take me off this high
Again I was expecting your call
But this time I didn't wait alone
Me and my phone
Have become friends again
He called,
And I question myself—is it a sin
To love to hear someone say,
"You're so beautiful"
In the most sincere way
And want to introduce me to friends as "my baby."
Is it a sin to enjoy every moment
Of his baritone phone voice,
And even indulge
While still the back
Of my mind you hold
(or even the front left corner)
Come out whenever you want to…

I'm Special

I've been told I'm special
He wants to make all my
Dreams come true
I dream of you
He says I need to be loved
He wants to give me everything
Your love; the only thing I want
He can't bring
He says I need to be *made love to*
The *right* way
He wants to fulfill my every fantasy
I fantasize about you night and day

You ask me not to leave
Then you don't call me for a week
But yet you "love" me
What am I supposed to think?

I think I'm in this alone
You don't know how to love me
I just need some attention
From the only one I see
As special
Who I want to give everything
Fulfill every dream and fantasy
You.

Reminders

Reminders of Him everywhere,
His cousin down the street.
The reason He's gone today
that our lips happened to meet.
sweet, sweet lips
cold, cold heart
speaks when he sees me
no guilt for breaking my heart
or for leaving me
with the knife set deep—
in my back
in His back
in my heart, in my heart
I just want to SCREAM
when I see that double-edged sword of a smile
all the while, laughing at my ignorance
my stance is unsure
He is unaware of my existence.
Dizzy from memories of Him,
it's too bad you're so much alike.
I just want to go back, take my lips away,
say goodnight.
I thought I was kissing Him
in my mind, I was
with my eyes closed, heart open
teardrops falling in my ears
thought we'd finally been reunited
(after all these years)
I was wrong—all feeling gone
until…
that double-edged sword of a smile
reminds me of my sin
and this nauseous feeling of loneliness
reminds me of Him.

Love Poem 3

There is a knife
slowly cutting my heart
       Into little pieces
stabbing
       pulling back
stabbing
       pulling back
I am in excruciating pain
I'm nauseous

I am in love

again

all by myself.

Plea of Insanity

For you I'd run a thousand miles
and swim a thousand seas

For you I'd forget my name
and hope you'd remember me

For you I'd take back everything
and redo it all again

For you I'd go back in time
and take back every sin

Take me back.

Love Poem 4

When I am happy
I am on the highest
      of highs
touching the skies
soaring with open heart
closed eyes

(we all know where that got me before)

When I am sad
I reach rock bottom
swimming in pools of
      salty tears
darkness nears
I get scared,
in fright—
I suck it up and
      hastily run back
      towards that dim light
the cycle continues.

Blue Moon

"What's up?
How are you?"
In my mind, thinking;
'Why'd you call me,
out of the blue?'
I mean—I want to talk
but I don't.
I want to say, 'I love you,'
but I won't.
A few months ago
I really wanted you to call
but now after so long,
after hiding what's inside—
I don't know if I can be strong
I don't know if I can hide,
it had gotten a little easier,
to lie to myself—
say the feelings were gone,
say I could be by myself,
but then you call out of the blue—
take those feelings off the shelf,
dust them off—
polish them for yourself,
then you leave and leave me
questioning what to do,
while I wait patiently for you and
for the next blue.

Yet Again

So, yet again
You've found your way in
Told me everything I want to hear
I have to believe you
Because I want it too much to lose faith
The traces of your betrayal
Are almost gone
No more visual aides to haunt
And haunt
And haunt
Me
While I sleep
While I work
And even while I play
I need you to stay
I need to believe
What you say
If I don't I'll go insane

Not His Type

Memories of love have faded now.
The evils now reside in his space.

The dream was shattered
when the one who said he'd always be there for me
came back with I'm not his type anymore.
'Not your *type?*'
I didn't think love was a type.
Maybe I've been watching too many
Beauty and the Beasts' or listening
to too many Cinderella stories…
but I thought love was forever.
Work through, grow through,
love—throughout it all.
But yet again I was wrong.
Yet again all feeling is gone.
But, no more nauseous feelings of loneliness,
just an empty heart that can stand no more pain,
no more feelings,
no more emotion—
I am a feeling-less existence,
some sort of being who is not heartless
but just less heart.
If I could feel,
I'd be too scared to think that I could ever
love again.

Letter to My Last Love

I sit in silence
rewind, fast forward
pause
my last love
9 seconds of my life
it was meant to be eternity
yet my heart yearned
for more
and I wasn't enough for you
so, the silence magnifies

9 seconds

it feels like an eternity
of pain
and I wonder…

Not a Dream

I sit around and wait
for you to call and say,
'I was just playing' or
for me to wake up and
call you and say,
'I just had the worst dream'
but it never happens and
here I sit writing
and thinking
thinking and writing
about you

sealing the validity
of this reality
that you don't want me
anymore.

I Hate You

I hate you—
I want to hate you even more everyday.
I hate you.
I want to say, "You make me sick,
stupid dick, I hate you!"
(but I can't, because we don't talk)
I want to say, "Stop calling me!"
(but I can't because you don't
and I'm not even a thought)
I hate you.
I want to say, "Leave me alone,
get out of my life!"
(but you're already gone)
I hate you,
because you've done me wrong
I hate you,
because I love you and you're gone.
I hate you,
because you've left, but you won't
leave my head.
I hate you, I hate you, I hate you!
And I'll hate you until I'm dead.

Love Poem 5

My heart is being ripped
into two halves
and he's on both sides
pulling and yanking
slowly tearing it apart
but he says he never meant
to hurt me and
that is what they always say
Is that supposed to ease
my pain or their guilt?
I am always the one left
feeling this way.
Soon,
I will no longer feel.

Pain

I'm done—
done writing all this "good" poetry about you.
I'm through.
No more bestsellers feasting off my pain,
reveling in my discomfort,
placing sunshine on my rain.
I worked hard for these emotions,
put in good time for this hurt.
These are the results of all my trust and all my
faith—
all the work.
So, let me keep my pain for awhile,
forget letting it all out,
it's mine—no doubt.
But it seems everyone who hears "your" poem
wants to comfort it all away—
let her stay.
Me and pain have known each other so long,
we are beginning to be friends,
now you want me to send her away
with all these silly poems,
No More!
I don't need to release,
I don't need any friends,
only to be subjected to this vulnerability again—
only to lead to more pain in the end?
Might as well get used to her being around,
I've found her some good use.
Pain is my guard protecting my heart from
moving on to anyone else,
protecting my heart from being sucked into the trap
and from being seduced,
basically, protecting my heart from loving another
you.

The End

My feelings have changed
I mean the love is the same
but I'm no longer willing to
be made a fool of again
and again
and again
that's it
I'm done
I mean I love the feeling of
our bodies
as one
but our minds don't align
as they should
oh…
why do I still wish they would?

Cliffhanger

Everyday I came to visit you @ that cliff
('that cliff' being a state of mind)
I would visit in thought or even in the physical,
leaving my real world far behind.
We would sometimes look down @ the water,
and say how beautiful it would be to jump again,
but then I'd say, "Never mind."
One day you pushed me to the edge of the cliff,
forcing me to jump with you or to run away,
I ran back to my new life where I know what's to come,
the water might be too cold to stay.

(It's not safe down there.)

I can't visit you on that cliff anymore.
It's just not safe, can't you see?
For one day I might go and just happen to fall in,
then what would become of me?
I've been down there before and I almost drowned,
had to learn to swim and break free.
But, all the while I was waiting,
waiting for you to come and save me.

"I can't breathe," I yelled, "I need your help!"
I wanted you to teach me to swim.
But, you weren't ready yet, you didn't oblige,
now I'm @ that cliff again.

I am consciously choosing safety.

I am running away… again.

Keyboard

Right now my mind
is like a keyboard
and you are dancing wildly
on the keys
no rhythm
no consistency
it's like cluttered noise
and I can't stand it
can you please unplug this
keyboard?
(maybe you should think
of playing the guitar)
it's funny because
I just realized
I am the one
holding the cord.
Unplugged…

chapter 2

when did you see the butterflies again…

A Woman's Mind
(behind the mystery)

Sometimes a girl just needs to be held really tight
and told things she just might be able to believe.

Sometimes a girl just needs to know she's wanted
around and missed when she's not.

Sometimes a girl just needs to know she's wanted
for more than sweating in six different positions and
just needs to be told she has good conversation and
looks good too.

Sometimes a girl just needs and doesn't get.

So, instead of leaving
she just keeps grabbing
and showing her loyalty
through nights of long hours of feel good
to make up for what's missing.

All she really wanted was a hug.
But, she gets on top
to take a ride on life
until she dreams

'maybe one day he'll come around'

Fool

yet again I play the role
of the broken hearted
fool
swimming in pools
of salty tears
wishing someone
would fill me in on the rules
because playing the fool
is getting old beyond its years

Past

there used to be
a time
we fit together
my warm space
felt like home to
you, to
me
there used to be
a time
you had this power
over me
you controlled my
thoughts
but that time is
gone
I will no longer
play that role

Maybe

I thought of you tonight
and for the first time
in a while
the stomach ache was gone
in fact, it never showed itself
I realized tonight
I just might
be over you
I still wonder what you're doing
how you are treating life
with your independence
strength
oh, I know you're alright
I thought about you tonight
not an everyday thing anymore
every other day

I wonder how you are

Maybe.

Borrowed Love

As we begin on this journey
of desires to fulfill
Remember as we lay
that a woman I am still
No matter how well I know
the truth of what we do
I will pretend, until my hearts content
that I am in love with you
And please, to me,
this favor oblige
As we touch and caress
and you look into my eyes
Allow me, if only for one moment,
to believe
That the one you truly are in love with
is me.

I Need *You*

He did everything right
He said everything he was
supposed to say
As I snuggled under his arm
with my eyes closed
It became painfully obvious
that I could not pretend
I sniffed and cried
Cried and sniffed,
"It's not you," I said.
It's not *you.*

Oprah Episode

I don't know how
to fall in love
I don't know how
to let go
I don't know how
to break down the walls
I don't know how
to know
(and knowing is half
the battle)

Mr. Right

Window stains are all I see
As I stare in search of you
Fingerprints and watermarks
(this is all I ever do)
You're never here
I'm never there—
(Where you are)
Its true
That I'd give up my life
And all things nice
Just to wait for you.

Crush

Every time
You step into a room
I steal your energy
And make it mine
Every time

Every time
I am in your presence
I am temporarily blinded
By your shine
Every time

Every time
You glide across the floor
Everything stands still in my mind
And I am stuck on that one moment in time
Every damn time!

So, when are you going to notice me?

Innocence

He reminds me of someone I've seen before—
The anxiousness in his voice as he speaks
The certain uncertainty—
The way he licks his lips,
And I smile.
He reminds me of something
Sort of like that new crush feeling
That goes away without you even realizing it,
But its existence is always recognized
From the outside and remembered
And keeps hope alive for the future
He reminds me, yes of—
Of the look that would be framed
And hung on the wall of my heart…
Innocence.
He reminds me
Of all the things I miss and
Things I've never even seen,
Rolled up into a hopeless feeling
Of what I would want to be.
He reminds me of— of…
Of Love.

Patience

I could feel the electricity
From across the room
And our eyes met
A gentle voice spoke gentle words
As the crimson blaze took over my face
And I do not regret
What I said next surprised me too
"I want you,
Not next week, not tomorrow—
Right now!"
But somehow I did not realize I
Said it all in my head
And I was wondering if the expression
On my face could be read
Because his eyes
His eyes had smiles that danced like
Rain on the three rivers
And I smiled too
Thinking, "If he only knew!"
But I didn't say
I just played the cool role
And allowed my mind to race
Because the angel on my left shoulder
Said, "You've got all the time in the world,
Be patient, wait."

I Want You

I want bittersweet kisses
With morning breath
Hot, sweaty afternoon sex
I wanna fall asleep with you
Lyin' on my chest
I want you
Still inside me
Sticky and nasty
There is no substitute
This is the way it has to be
Sunday through
Every Saturday
I want you
To cum inside my walls
To pulsate in between my thighs
I want you to talk me into a mental high
If you try
I'll try
I want you
To want me so bad
We'll do it on my cycle
And a couple of other freaky things
I'd like to do
I want us to build together,
there's nothing to decipher—
I WANT YOU!
(and believe me baby,
I get what I want)

Sleep

i wanna fall asleep
as if i'm falling in love
slow, and easy
(with the lights on)
i want my eyes to start
wide open watching tv
and gently shut in a
slow, almost fluid motion
with grace
like i'm making love
i wanna get to the point
right before sleep but
after total consciousness
and peacefully fantasize
my way into sheer bliss
moaning in ecstasy
i want to fall asleep with you

Butterflies and Caterpillars

Right now we have butterflies
And I want caterpillars
And I want to give him caterpillars too
Because butterflies…
Just won't do.

You see, caterpillars mean
I'm on his mind from 10 to 2
(and even the in between)
(lacing his dreams through and through)
But butterflies…
Just won't do.

You see, butterflies mean a crush
And caterpillars make you feel brand new,
Especially because they include the words,
"I Love You."
So, butterflies…
Just won't do.

You see, "we" is us and "him" is you,
And I think…. Well I know….
No— I am…
In love with you.
That's why butterflies…
Just won't do.

I am in Love

"Baby,
if loving you ain't right…
then the wrong thang's what I'm gon' do,
'cause ain't no loving unless I'm loving you."

I'm smiling when I lay myself down to sleep
To when I wake up—
I'm thinking about you
I'm going to tell you what's on my mind
I'm totally in love with you

At first, it just seemed as if my crush wouldn't go away—
no matter what I'd do
do you feel me?
'cause I feel you
just wanna be near you
so I can smell you
so I can hear you—
breathe!
"God—
please breathe!"

I am suffocating from this intoxicating air you bring into my world.
I am drunk off your sweetness, your sex appeal.
You've got me saying things I've got way too much pride to say.
For real—you bring out my alcoholic tendencies—
I need a sip of your love @ least 3 to 4 times a day.
I get a buzz off your touch—
You've given me temporary insanity!

Please don't be temporary.
I want to be drunk and insane all my life.
I don't need to think logically for myself—
As long as you can think for me twice.

This isn't me—
simply put.
These aren't things I'd say or
something I'd do.
But I simply can't put these
feelings into words
because I simply
love you.

If

If you were the sky,
I would want to be the clouds that dwell in you.
If you were the grass,
I would want to be the soil from which you grow.
If you were hurting from holding in,
I would want to be your heart's surrender.

I just want to love you
I want you to know

If you were here and I was there,
I would want to be here with you.
Through good and bad, thick and thin
The "if" will pull us through

Your Love

lover—
you breathe, speak, sweat, exemplify—
love
in your presence i am suffocating from
the sweet aroma of love
drunk off of the air your love brings
your love sings a soothing melody and
rocks me to sleep @ night
your love dances a rhythm-ous tango
that my body can't fight
your love reads like a racy love story
that i want to read all day
your love, your love
may i have a taste—of your love
please!?
just a sample i can keep tucked away
under my pillow
safe from love haters, hate lovers
may i reap the benefits of
your love
feel the soulful, silky, inside rumble
of your love
can you bring those butterflies
around my door, just once more?
just once more—*i promise.*

Happy Birthday

I want to feel every inch of you
Inside my domain of love
And I am willing to do anything you ask
To receive all of the above
You turn me inside out
And make me feel things I've never felt
You give me an orgasm straight from heaven
And for real—I don't want anyone else
To touch me, to look @ me, or to even say my name
Because I know that if it's not you loving me
Baby, it just isn't quite the same
So, just do what you please to me
Give of yourself in any way
Because, I want nothing but to please you
And be pleased
Happy Birthday

Bliss

He kissed me for what seemed
like an hour, but couldn't have
been more than three to seven
minutes.

It was bliss.

Upon that moment,
I would commence to be
wrapped around
his little finger
(or any other finger he
wanted, for that matter)

Simple

Last night
as we lay
he lightly caressed
my arm
as he talked
about things that
didn't really matter
(but mattered)
and as my head
rest
on his chest
there was no other
place in this world
that I wanted to be.

Dreaming

I dreamt about you last night
and a sweet, sweet dream it was
I didn't want to wake to begin
a new day
just wanted to stay
stay, stay
in that dream forever
though I couldn't even see
your face
you had my time and space
I'd wonder who this person is
making my insides
feel new
yet there's just no time
because all thoughts
begin and end @ you—and me
I don't even know what we
did in this dream
I just know—*I* was @ peace
you, me
everything in between
Sun, Moon, Stars, Earth
as a matter of fiction
the whole Galaxy
but, none of that matters
nothing even matters
except you and me.

chapter 3

a gallon of rocky road...

Raped

what was once precious to me
has now been stripped away
trashed
like yesterday's newspaper
every time I see
what was once precious to me
I bleed
and rekindle all the pain
inside, I cried and still cry
and will even cry more
but I will eventually stop crying
the lock on my souls door
is still intact

30 Minutes, Press Start

I'm on the verge of destruction
And I don't feel like I'm in control
Someone is pulling my strings and
Pushing my buttons with no compassion
Testing the breaking point,
@ what level of heat will I boil
and bubble and spill over into the
endless, bottomless pit of the microwave?
I want to cut the strings and kill the computer
But I can't find the scissors
And right now the microwave seems to be
Smarter than me, (and I know I'm smart)
Maybe I should just get checked out,
Take some magic candy that will
Make me see stars and flowers and
Forget that I'm in the microwave
But I'll take the high road and just
Keep trying to talk myself out of
A chemical imbalance and chalk it up
To being my destiny,
My curse,
To being crazy, insane
Misunderstood,
Just press cancel on the microwave and end it all.

Insane

He said I was borderline insane
and
He said I was crazy
and
here I sit with
the knife and pill bottles
in hand
dying—
I mean trying to prove them
wrong
but its not working
slowly I run the blade over my
wrist
(vertically—remember they say that's
the best way)
and as the sharpness breaks the skin
I sigh
I don't have to lie to myself
anymore
I am crazy
and while I pop some pills
I can relive every moment
of temporary insanity
because its real now.

Suicide Gone Wrong

my blood clots too fast to kill myself
(I just found that out)
and my hearts too strong to just die out from pills
so, basically I'm stuck here without a gun
(I'm a nut!)
the nurse thinks it's "pretty cool" and "pretty neat"
that *I* write poetry
(how funny—
now the whole world will patronize me)
(is this what I asked for or what)
wow—if my mom could see me now, she'd cry
the doors are wide open
and I'm naked with a pen and a pad
how sad it is that I couldn't have just died last night
I'm just alive with a new bill to add to my
collection
I guess when the bill collectors call, I'll say,
"not to my recollection"
I should have just went away
what will my family think of me
I'll just be an embarrassment
(wait, now the doctor wants me to talk to a
"specialist")
specialize in what, fixing a nut?
or maybe paying all my bills
or forcing people to love me like they say they will
or maybe he'll just specialize in making himself
think
I've changed my mind and decided its okay to live
in hell,
but I won't, I don't want to be here
I just want to start the game over
try all over again from the beginning
(now my "specialist" is talking to someone,

and they are looking right @ me)
I feel like a lab rat and I'm in a glass box
where everyone can see in and they don't even give thought
to the fact that I can see out too
I can see every glance and *"crazy girl in that room"* thing they do
well, blood work presides and I must give my arm back
(damn, last night the blood didn't run like that!)
turns out I had just missed
the big boy, fat vein
I think I'm truly insane
because I can sit here and put on a great act
of being "okay" and "a great person" in fact

maybe I'm a crazy, genius, with insane qualities?
Or maybe I give myself too much credit
and life is just getting the best of me.

Where am I?

He said I had his mind
And that was more than having his heart
He handed me the plant with a vase and said,
"I wanted to put it together but…"
And in my mind everything was silent,
Everything was okay
He gave me a plant and a nervous smile
He wanted to make me feel better
He said that he learns so much from *me*, everyday
And that's why he loves *me* so much
Because he's wanting to be tender for me
The master of truth and bluntness
Wants to be tender for *me*?
I cried.
I cried for the things I've wished for
I cried for the love
I cried for the walls falling in front of me
I cried for what wasn't enough
I cried for the "*us*" that I wanted so much
I cried for what couldn't be
But, mostly I cried for giving up his heart
for the ongoing search for
me.

Suicidal Tendencies

When the suicidal tendencies are on the other foot,
The foot of someone you love,
How do you understand?
How do you give counsel when every other day it
Runs through your mind—
"The Master Plan to the End"
I don't want to go anymore
She needs me and I need her
So how do I get her to stick around?
How do I get her to forgive me for my broken promises
And long absences…
For the many chances…
For all the things that have happened…
How do I get her to forgive me for all the time
I wasn't there during the hard times in her life…
For not being there as she contemplated with a knife…
How do I get her to forgive me for breaking a strong trust
In hopes that I would be saving her life?

a gallon of rocky road...

the house is cold
even though its warm outside
(a cold house is not much
to want to come home to)
the chill you left behind
stains my dreams with icicles
and yet my heart is still
warm for you

Trials of Love

Why is love treating me like a stepchild
And why does pain know my number by heart
Loneliness calls me by my nickname
And regret, (let's not even start)
Love won't take me home to meet the parents
Pain already did
Right after lust took me to the bedroom
And asked if he could "hit"
When I said yes because love doesn't notice me
And joy doesn't know my name
I settled for getting to know orgasm personally
Love didn't show up, but @ least I came!

changing the pillowcase…

tears line the rims of my eyes
and mark my pillow with memories
of my heart's discontent under disguise
and my pillow being the only friend to me

Remembering Love

I remember the way he used to study my body
like it was a work of art.
He had memorized every curve
my feet he kissed and named *his* feet
I remember how he would kiss the crease where my
leg ended and my butt began, he named that *his* spot
But I was not in love
and I remember.
I remember when I met him it had been so long
since anyone had caressed me
and he appreciated me
I remember him cooking breakfast with me
and giving me the remote
He respected me yet I begged him to make love to
me
I remember the look on his face from across the
restaurant table
from across the bedroom as I took my tour
and I remember his face as he sat beside me
at the bus stop waiting for the 74A
and I had to tell him, "I am not in love."
I remember
I still see the pain in his eyes as he said, "I know,
but I love you anyway." and he said he'd known all
along
but he still wanted to be in my presence
still wanted to give me everything.
I remember he still wrote to me
letters of dreams of saving all of his money
to move across three states to be near me
dreams I remember
dreams of love
But I was not dreaming, because I was not in love
and I remember.

Not So Many Words

In not so many words
He said he loved me
And in not so many words I had to relay
That my feelings are not the same
In not so many words.
I led him on
Because I was lonely,
And it had been so easily done to me
(but in not so many words)
I led a good brother to my
Bermuda Triangle
Only for him to be lost and
Swallowed up and
I didn't throw him a life jacket
I didn't try to save him
Because I needed him to
Tell me how warm the water was
I needed him to tell me how good it felt
I needed him to swim in my pool,
Just so he could remind me that I was and
Still am *alive*!
But now I'm dead.
(in not so many words)
because my conscience has come to lay claim
and the rocks are crying out
because I was wrong
and I knew it all along
I knew I was hurting someone
And pushed care aside
For the almighty *"I"*
Being selfish and now
I cry.

Release (Multiple Times)

I've decided to leave you alone
And it's okay
It doesn't even hurt to say goodbye

you don't know me @ all
and you don't really want to get to know
who I am
but it's okay
because I never really gave a damn
I got what I wanted
And I wasn't trying to get to know you
I just wanted some release (multiple times)
And I think that's all you wanted too
So, now that we both got what we wanted
I've decided to leave *you*.

Truthfully

They say, "The truth will set you free."
And I hope that rings true
Because I am bearing my soul to you,
Truthfully—
I'm not perfect
(Nor will I ever be)
I am not even as strong as you might perceive me to be.
I am not always happy.
(Even when I carry a smile.)
I'm not always the best friend I can be
I slack every once and a while
But truthfully,
I am human.
I am a good person.
I do try my best most of the time
But please don't judge my actions
Judge my heart
Because, sometimes my heart can't make up my mind

Same Difference

in the beginning
they all seem different
and yet the same
different from the one
before
but the same as the one
before the change
so, when does the difference
become the same,
through every name
change or
game change?

Thoughts On: Focus

I was in the office the other day
And this guy was on the phone
And I heard him say, "What you focused on?"
And then this girl, who's known him longer
Than me said, "Oh, a new chick, I see!"
And he said, "Yeah! A new one."
She said, "I know, because you're not worried about
What someone is focused on!"
And she was right.
So, I was on the phone later that night
And this guy I barely knew asked me
To spend the night
And I wondered to myself, "to see what I'm
Focused on, right?"

Not Naïve

He confessed his
Infatuation with me
And I,
I listened as he said how beautiful
I am
I listened as he made it known how much
He misses me
I listened as he told me that the
Perfect wife would be me
I listened intently
And I,
I said, "Thank you."

Thoughts On: Relations

For so long I mistook one for the other
And now after experiencing the truth
I no longer mistake one for the other
I just accept that they are not the same
And do it anyway
Because it feels so good! (momentarily)
Satisfaction, power *then* empty
(But the power and satisfaction definitely
come first)
Oops—Time to re-up again!

Thoughts On: Money and People

"People who have been constantly catered to, need to prove something to make up for or to compensate for what they are lacking, that is why you got screamed on in front of everyone. It is up to you to weigh out the risks versus the reward, to decide whether you should stay in that position. Can you deal with people's ignorance and mental inferiority and at the same time remain yourself without stooping to that level? Sure stooping feels good with the immediate gratification but it won't last long…"

I Don't Know How to Write a Poem Anymore

I don't know how to write a poem anymore
The words used to flow like silk in a soft spring breeze
But now, it's like a hundred degree summer with the same silk dress
(It's kind of sticky)
I don't know how to write a poem anymore
Because a poem should have imagery and color and texture
And I don't know how to do that
I just know how to feel
How to feel vibrant
Like a yellow and white linen sundress on a Sunday afternoon
Or sad…
Sad like dirty clothes forming a mountain in my room and no motivation
Or just how to feel easy…
Easy like a calm breeze coming off the clear blue water
With tropical fish swimming in schools
So, I just won't write a poem anymore
I'll write about my confused feelings
And scattered joy and even
The pain, purple like a lingering
Bruise
That's just what I'll do
Because
I don't know how to write a poem anymore.

chapter 4

singing in the shower...

Singing in the Shower

If you could sing
would you sing all day?
Would you sing until
your day was bright
and your heart was smiling?
Would you sing your blues away?

I would,
I would sing my blues away.

Time

I heard a sound
emotion spilled from the depths
could it be:
could it be… him?
but it wasn't
I saw a vision
pressure burst the trapped heart
could it be?
could it be...
and it was,
the morn of a new day
my savior!

Optimism

sunlight
replenishing
my strength
dawn's healing;
unobtrusively entering
my wingspan
dreams of castles and
carriages disappear
reality of life
seeps through
endless possibilities
situational awareness says,
"I AM ALIVE!"
I can feel the sunlight
replenishing
my strength
dawn's healing

Live

When you laugh,
Laugh like it's your last
When you cry,
Cry with conviction
And when you love,
Love to no end—
And that's living!

Breath Control

When the clock moves too slow
And patience is on crack
I breathe.

Happiness

Do I choose happiness or does happiness choose me?
If the latter is so,
I'm sick and tired of being left out.

Passionate

Sometimes passion whispers
sweet nothings in your ear
While @ other times he explodes in
song

Sunny Days

Don't let your dreams fade away
With the dawn or evaporate in the sun.
Let them forever run on like a waterfall,
Forever run on and on.

Zonin'

I hear the music
And it's like…
I slip into a zone

Soothing

Slow

Relaxing

I know I need this
No more worries
No more cares

I'm off
In a land
Where there's…
No anything

Except me
And my music

Deception

the green grass
on the other side
is as succulent
as the apple of Eve

the analogy—
they all deceive

Tanka

homeless winter tears
only salt on cheeks remain
dirty visions to
bundled dreams of not the same
while ten percent goes to God

Tanka

prison of secrets
atrium bars lock the mind
how does truth break free?
thus I out of misery
but now I eat sour grapes

Tanka

Naïve. Now I live
within a diamond clustered
heart, just because you
can see your reflection, that
does not mean you are welcome.

Tanka

Mr. Belvedere,
In summer heat, sometimes I
drink liquid fire
and flame just to close my eyes
and pretend… passionately.

Tanka

On weekends he goes
out of town to drown out this
perceived poverty
and I patiently await
return… because we—have dreams.

Tanka

hurricane season
and my heart is on the shore
twisting with each wind
drowning @ high tide, candle-
lit self help says to detach

(1)

silence streams gentle
touches of light and darkness
through bright muffled sound
and bares all truth
(I am only one)
inhale, exhale—breathe rhythmically
thoughtlessly living fantasies and
nightmares in reality
while the darkness breathes silence
that paints colors through sound
and bares all truth
(I am only one)
the loudness of light sweats distinct
sound, in which silence is gaseous-ly
given off, one by one by one
atom @ a time
and the silence of sound
bares all truth
(I am only one)

you can hear the mood change
in a perfect silence
so silence and sound coexist
light breezes and dark moods
breathe silent kisses of life
that can be heard around the world
baring all truth
(We are only one)

Haiku

pray for forgiveness
for my human tendencies
with hate in my heart

chapter 5

if the walls could talk...

Mental Stimulation

He licked my toes, rubbed my calves,
even ran is fingers up and down my inner thighs
but, he did not stimulate my mind
He kissed me ever so softly on my neck
and was always willing to grind
but, he did not make my toes curl,
did not send shivers up my spine,
did not motivate blackberry after thoughts
because he did not stimulate my mind
He didn't speak on spirituality or say,
fuck the world and speak on knowledge and truth
He did not try to lead me anywhere *except* to the bedroom
I needed a king to guide me to the Promised Land
so, I could follow from night into day
because, see, I believe if you put the right man in your life
it's okay for the marriage vows to say "obey"
(no omissions necessary)

You see, he would say all those things a man is
supposed to say to make me moist
but, he did not stimulate my mind
and that left me with no choice—but to leave
because I need realness, I need a strong mind
with strong opinions and strong views
Someone who doesn't believe everything whispered in his ear
or spoken loudly on the news
(Negative Energy Will Sell)
I need a man who will read 3 books and still be thirsty or uneasy
Until he's read 3 more books or @ least discussed the other 3 with me

He wants my point of view and views me as his queen
He knows he does not *have to* but chooses to come home to me
because, like me—
he can't see it any other way

Golden Sandalwood

My lover is a combination of
Bob Marley, Marcus Garvey, and
A touch of Steve Harvey
But so much more in my eyes
Because in fact and in truth
His youth is only a sign of magnificent
Growth to come
He is the one divine, supreme being
Sent to my life by the Creator
His power has me wanting to shower
Him with love, adoration, and patience
I want to have His children
I want Him to father me
He teaches me in every conversation
We carry, and I, never grow weary
He says He wants to bring fruits and
Vegetables to the table and I say
With every breath He takes in my presence,
I am fed.

More than bread alone
But a feast of knowledge and information
That's what I'm tasting, not wasting a bit
Eating everything on my plate
Feelings of, "I can't wait for my next meal,
I want it now!"
A glutton
Somehow never getting full off of this
Tree of Life or ever getting enough

Golden Sandalwood and dread oil
Bathe my sheets and my heart
The only things stained are the
Undergarments thrown wildly about the room

He has written His name in Black
Permanent marker, all over my essence
And when we love
I wonder how anyone else
Could ever have made an attempt

Love @ 1st Sight

He smiled,
I sighed...
Both wanting what we want right now!
No exceptions, but rejections possible appearance
Leaves both silent, in another world
Where love @ 1st sight does exist
Where everything and nothing is missed
No place is left untouched
Everyplace touched wanting more and more
But silence separates hearts, bodies, and minds
Time cannot replace that 1st moment
Both are left with regret because what goes on
In the imagination
Would only be met with competition
Going the extra mile
For awhile they stare from across the room
Catching stray glances and waiting for the next
move
But in the back of the mind you'll find
The fear of the possibility
Rejection will get the best of me
And he
So we
Sit
And
Flirt
From across the room
Thinking, "Is he playing with my mind?"
"If I go over will it be too soon—
she might be running game."
"There's no way he could be thinking the same...
as me."
"I'll wait—we'll see—
she'll be here tomorrow."

"Damn! I have to go and I can't come back—
I'm giving the hints he just won't follow!"
Oh, well, that's where we end.
Love came and went before it even had a chance to begin.
The end.

Warning Label

I've heard it said that her smile could brighten the
darkest of days
Radiating brighter than even the sun's rays
She is as sharp as a double-edged sword
Cutting both ways
Because, simultaneously someone is falling in love
And someone is going through pain
Realizing he can never have her—
She cannot be contained

She is the fire that will warm you up
When the cool breeze is just too much
She brings electricity and chemistry with the
slightest touch
She carries a certain cosmic power as well as an air
of mystery
While it may seem as if she's an open book
You cannot see me
My fire cannot be contained
It will run through your life and wreak havoc
(Good and bad)
But when the ashes settle and the cinders cool
The day will be sad
I cannot be contained

You'll get to know me but you never *know* me until
I'm gone
All preconceived notions of who I am will have
been wrong
That person is not her, its only one side of me
One of my many alternate personalities
But she is required to go
Me—you are never really supposed to know
I am a mystery to science and logic

Divine intervention to be exact
An angel of some sorts, maybe
But not the soul mate that you lack
Warning: DO NOT GET ATTACHED
I will bring out sides of you that you never knew you had
Or the ones you locked up long ago
But it is you—yourself, not me,
Whom you really should get to know

I cannot be contained

Déjà vu

I heard laughter in the distance,
I stayed on the path, it was rough, dark
(And fear was beginning to get the best of me)
But I heard laughter in the distance
So, I let the darkness guide me
I began to get used to the thorns
And my screams became muted,
Rather instead I began to sing
To make time pass more smoothly,
To combat the negative thoughts
Rising from the trail's harsh terrain
I still heard laughter in the distance
And I thought,
"What if they're laughing at me?"
Out of nowhere I tripped on a branch
That didn't seem to be there before
(But I wouldn't know, besides—it was dark)
As I was standing to brush myself
I thought back to that time…
And it made me smile
I continued back on my journey
With a smile because
I heard laughter in the distance
And I miss laughing
So, I decided to move faster,
My instincts and reflexes were kicking in
And before I knew it, I realized
I didn't hear laughter anymore
(What am I going to do? That was my light, my motivation.)
Before these thoughts had time to resonate
I came across two people along the way
The first person said… and before I

Could say anything
The second person said…
And I laughed so hard I forgot where I was
And then I stopped—
This situation reminded me of something,
So much that I couldn't think about anything else…

Translucent

I'll never be the same
But deep down, under all the confidence,
Before you get to the self-pride
And self-love,
Preceding the beautiful façade
Of a well put together woman,
I want to be.
(The same, that is.)
But, I will never be,
No matter my claim to this race, this culture,
My claim to "blackness"
I'll never fit in
And in order for me to make it
From day to day without exploding
I have to hide my feelings of self-hate
So that I don't force my internal burden onto others,
For their sake, not mine
But they don't see nor will they
Ever understand my plight.
"*Damn!* You're translucent!"
Those were the words he said boldly.
As if I don't look at myself
In the fucking mirror everyday
Like I don't see myself and cry sometimes
Because of the pain of not looking on the outside
how I see myself on the inside.
An unseen pain that hurts so much
I will never be like him,
I will never see or feel his pain first hand,
But his pain is accepted and mine is rejected.

Get over it, Nic, you think you've got it rough?
"Well, I'm sorry, I am not white
Nor do I seem to be black enough."

is she gone foreva?

this good girl has gone bad
and she can't seem to find herself
behind the flirtatious smile, the seductive eyes
there lies a girl—a young woman
with a heart that has been hurt, has seen hurt
has given hurt and now only knows how to flirt
to hide the pain of the *right* ones not loving her
no words of compassion change her insides
because inside she feels as if she's dying
she knows what she did last night
and the pain she carries swelters within
the fulfillment was short lived
but through men's attention she lives
through every smile and line of her beautiful eyes,
she decides to give life one more try,
with every speech on how her poetry is so moving
when she knows no one really understands
she plans to allow life one more chance,
one more chance to hurt her before she walks away
for the last time (as if life was a man)
because no one deserves to hurt her
this many times and get away with it
(not even life itself)
but then *he* stares as if he's never seen such a sight
in his life and she puts the pain up on the shelf
and thinks, "Maybe tomorrow I'll kill myself—
because *today,* today he's never seen
someone like me before in his life
and he said he's sure one day I'll be his wife."
so, for now she puts down the knife
and has a glimpse of hope for the future,
"I may be a wife!" she thought,
but he never really knew her,
and he never really tried

and once again she cries,
she tries to dry her eyes
with optimism and positive self talk
but she's lost hope for the present
and that's the worst feeling of all
because she can't see the smiles of tomorrow,
she can't hear the laughter in the distance,
she can't feel the peace that comes from the struggle,
all she wants is the path with the least resistance,
but the path is hard to find because
she has yet to realize that all she has to do is decide
and life will open her eyes
and show her a brighter future
so what if *he* never really knew her
she's got to get to know herself
there in the heart of her soul lies her true wealth
babygirl has to decide who she wants to be
stop living for others approval and roll up her sleeves—
and get to work!

good girls gone bad don't have to be gone forever if we choose
we can certainly work up enough courage to guide ourselves back to the middle and stop allowing ourselves to be used
because, babygirl—he's going to keep taking it as long as you keep giving it first
but don't let any man or woman become the author of your self-worth
let your heart show you the way, because
no matter what your past looks like
there *is* hope for a better today

Soul Mate

though I don't know if I've ever met you
or if my eyes have ever grazed your face
what I do know is that I love you and you love me
and I will wait for you in this place
because...
I am feeling the emptiness beside me
as I lie restlessly in my bed
trying desperately to meet you in my dreams
yet you keep me up, on my mind instead
I have erotic daydream fantasies
that our minds will intertwine
(two intellectual bodies mingle amongst the few)
both enchanted by the others' words
(two of a different yet the same kind)
in this modern world of ignorance
this feeling is so new
I dream of our sensual passionate wills
uniting in just one meeting of the eyes
we'll speak on spirituality and the measure of
success after death
I'm left on a natural high
I see our spirits praying together
our bodies lying side by side
take a ride on these mental tides
don't drown in the world, black pearl
let your soul bathe in me
waves of imagination, eloquent expression and
sensitivity
from you I'll ask the brutal truths
hidden deep inside your heart and soul
from me you will get the world, with patience
that's how much power I hold

engulfed in your whole being

Our Story

Black and white stripes and Black Star
Birthed these crashing stars
And the cosmic encounters grew
From heated debates on love and marriage
To flirty free-styling on the cool evening beach,
Playing anxiously with innuendoes in the backroom
To eventually, with dismay, not even speaking
Only telepathically connected in thought
I—immersed in my poetry
He—engrossed in his rhymes
And together we made lines colorful
Beautiful black and spiritual green
Crimson passion red
Christening the first home of our love
Before there was a place to lay our heads
I wanted to carry geniuses in all shades of brown
With my personality and his mind
And his looks blended with mine
To create the best noun—
Perfection
Because in him I could see more than just my
reflection
I saw fire and revolution, hidden sensitivity
I saw tiny bits in him
That I wanted to piece together in me
To make 'we' a permanent combo
The steady rise of the crescendo always climaxed
on time
The fall was sometimes painful
But we always landed with our feet on the ground
Together
Even if only as the best of friends
This revolutionary process has no end because
I am his Ma'at and he is my Thoth

The Truth complemented with
The creator of writing and science
The most rewarding alliance
Forever to be reborn just to find each other

There will never be a better love poem written to replace our story.

A Poem For You, Brooklyn

My love for you
Doesn't hide in melodies
It doesn't even sleep
It sings in sister circles
Plays on your Brooklyn stoops
Dances down Fulton St.
My love for you
Doesn't compete
With any other love
It is peace in a time of war
You can find it
In the open windows of my heart
Or behind my brownstone door
My love for you
Can't contain you
But it can make buildings melt away
It can remove walls to allow you in but
My love will never force you to stay
My love for you
Doesn't scream out in anger
Only moans with pleasure and laughs
Sometimes even giggles with joy
Damn, I'm so blessed!
I will never say I never had enough
This much I say is true
My love and my life were made complete
In my love for you

Fuck You
(to all the "conscious" ones @ the poetry venue)

Fuck you
Because you're trying to be someone else
Trying to be one dimensional and I'm multifaceted
And want to stay that way, to be myself
So, fuck you
Because you don't think its cool that
One day I'm wearing a head-wrap and speaking about revolution
And the next night I'm out with a guy trying to seduce him
And two days ago I was @ the bar with a drink in my hand
And a week before that I was out with a different man
You know what, fuck you
Because you can judge all your life
Or you can live and realize—there is no wrong or right (it's all perception)
And I'm not going to live by your rules
Western civilization has tricked you into playing the fool
And into thinking you're better
When we all have the same human nature and tendencies down to the letter
So, fuck you
Because I didn't cut my hair because I'm "conscious"
I cut it because I wanted to
I don't care if you have a perm or keep your nappy roots
Maybe on day you'll realize it isn't about *your* hair,
The gear *he's* wearing or whether *she's* dark or light
That don't have shit to do with it

But your attitude just might!
Fuck you
Because it's not about the music you listen to
Or the things you like to say to someone when you're naked
It's not about whether you like to give pleasure or whether you're a taker
A lot of ya'll don't like *Jay-Z*
So, you don't think I should like him *either*
Well, maybe your conscious asses should listen a little deeper
 I didn't know conscious equaled out to shallow and judgmental these days
Maybe we need to all go home and look in the mirror and think of some ways
That we can stop FUCKING each other
And let some love in here!
Until then, no fear
Because believe me, I'm not going to be judged by your convictions, just my own
So, stop trying to change me and everyone else
Into what YOU WANT TO BECOME!

Damn. Fuck you.
Go read a book.

I Just Need You

I don't fucking need you!
I just *need* you…
I just need you…
I just need *you…*

But you don't even know me
Every time I see you
All you do is try to show me
How many ways you can stretch my legs
Or how many different ways you can ask for head
But you don't even make love to my mind
Even though you've fucked on every angle of my bed
As you've mangled my body in the wind
You haven't even inquired about the scars on my wrists
Yet, you're always forcing them to bend
Over… backwards just to please you
My feelings don't even make the top ten
When I say no, you say now
And how much you need me
But
I don't fucking need you
I just need you
But you don't even know me!

You never read between the lines
When it comes to what you could be doing for me
Unless it's something to benefit you in the end
Oh—now you can see!
Without your glasses on
How about turning the light around that third eye on?
Because its time for you to go to class

Learn something more about women
Besides tits and ass
Study the lines in our faces
Feel the vibrations of our pain
Meditate on the depth of our words
And *believe me*, we'll do the same

Please, get to know who I am
Because, though I don't fucking need you
I just need you man.

He Called

He called…

And so many things went through my head
I mean, it had been weeks since I was "talking" to someone
And months since I was actually *with* anyone
And only God knows how long it had been since I was touched
(I mean really touched)

So, I picked up the phone…

And you know we always had one of those relationships where
When you need me you call, and if I need you I'll answer
(vice versa was true the same)
And I needed that day

So, I went over…

And the anxiousness was always there
The nervousness always tingled inside
And the butterflies—
Oh, the butterflies flew with hope
Hope for something that matched my past visits
Something similar to other times well spent
Because, he always was good @ pretending
As was I

So, I undressed…

I took off the disguise that said everything was okay
And the façade that told a tale of being happy alone

I unmasked the lies and gave him the naked truth
And as I stood undressed before him,
He stood unclothed before me

So, we made love…

With other people in our minds
But we made love just the same,
Passionately, slow, sensuous—achingly real
As we always did
And for a moment, it was healing
Every pain; past, present, and future
But when it was over
And I was done making love to the one who loved me
I wondered as I replayed every stroke in my mind
How many keys does he dance on like mine?
How many sad love songs does his body play?
How many, not with me?
And once again I was alone

So, I went home…

As soon as we were done
Before the sweat had time to dry
Before the,
"I'm meeting my trainer in the morning so…"
And I thought about sleeping where I didn't have to sleep with someone's back turned to me
Where I didn't have to wonder
If the one next to me was thinking that
My work was done, and I could leave now
Where I could stack the pillows behind me
And put one between my legs
And dream.
Dream that my love had me wrapped so tight
Because he just couldn't let me go

So, I slept and slept…

And forgot all about how the night ended
And when my girlfriends asked I told them how perfect it was
And how he didn't miss one spot
And how we danced all night
And they were happy for me
And couldn't wait for it to happen for me again
I had lied so well, I fooled myself into believing that I couldn't wait either
But I did wait.
I waited and waited
Only God knows how long and…

He called.

Ricky

I believed in you—
I believed in you and me
I believed so much that I gave up everything
I put all faith in the things you said
Had no thoughts they'd fall through
Baby, I belieeeeved,
I believed in you

I handcuffed my heart to yours
With no plans of needing the key
But now I'm asking you to give it back
Because, you didn't believe in me

Baby, we had dreams of freedom—
Freedom beyond what money could buy
Even though we aren't together now
I know those dreams weren't built on lies
I mean—we traveled the world and pitched a tent
and even made love under the stars
And not once did you say it wasn't enough or that maybe you needed more

The Motherland called to us and we had plans to make our pilgrimage
Start our life together with the most sacred of our trips
But there we stood in silence, on the edge of what could be
And though I believed in you, baby
You didn't believe in me

Didn't you know it was the same me all along?
The one to whom you could say anything?
You must have forgotten because you left me
broken hearted thinking of what could've been

I want you to know that it's okay
That I went on our sacred trip alone
Because, baby, I believe in me,
I mean, I truly believe
And that's the most spiritual lesson I could've learned...

Lovers

We consumed liquid ecstasy,
Licking and sucking poetry off each other's skin.
Passion sang, cried out, even whispered sweet nothings,
As children were birthed with dreams and words.

We made love—
Love poetry, with syllables and innuendo,
And as the words danced slowly off our tongues,
We became one.

Three lovers of words became
One love of verbs, nouns, and predicates,
Not a sexual meeting—
But an intertwining of the minds,
Sensual wills united, defying space and time.
These borrowed capsules creating wonders
To be heard for years to come and come and come,
And we came… in unison—
Trinity and evolution.

i wanna be a poet

i wanna be free
 see
things in things
unseen
i wanna be
be
when
being
is not the thing to
be

i wanna be a poet
make
my own language
overstood
during sleep
understood
during hours of light
and when night strikes
i wanna be me
a poet

but they say i can't be
me
a poet
no degree plaques
lining the walls
of my overstanding
blocking the moons luminous resilience
no
big
word
poems
framing my life's achievements

with
glass
blocking water's adaptable
versatile
natural absorption
i have no thing
nothing
holding me back
so forever will
i wanna be a poet

Thank you for purchasing and reading this book.

For more information on the author go to:

www.honeyandvinegar.com

Janis Nicole Townsend is also a guest blogger at www.maddishohm.com and sometimes goes by her affectionate monikers Nikki White or Nikki Blanco (in her words, the nicknames refer to her different personalities.)

A Page in Everyday Life, Townsend's second poetry book to be released, will be available early 2010.

The author currently resides in Brooklyn, NY with a roommate, a dog, a blackberry and a Mac.

www.ingramcontent.com/pod-product-compliance
Lightning Source LLC
LaVergne TN
LVHW091307080426
835510LV00007B/395